Inside

A

Heart

By Dudley (CHRIS) Christian

A

Pause For Poetry ©

Publication

Acknowledgement:

Special thanks to my wife, Marilyn Christian for compiling, organizing and finalizing the books of my collections. Her photographing and editing skills were vital to all of my works.

ISBN: 978-0-9877501-3-6

First Edition March 2012
Revised Edition June 2017

Cover Photograph: Cabos San Lucas, Mexico © Marilyn Christian

<u>An Opening Word by the Author...</u>

Many people often ask:

"How do you write and do you have to often rewrite your material?"

I have long summed up my answer to the above with the following:

"A Word, the written word, small purveyor of a thought, so like a thought, once thought, cannot be recalled, so too, a word once writ, should need NOT be re-written, for with such licence, we would but change ... the very substance of the thought."

... DNC © 1970

Dudley (Chris) Christian founded and hosted the first and only "PAUSE FOR POETRY" show dedicated solely to the introduction of new and unknown poets and their works. This TV series ran from 1974 to 1985.

Table of Contents

Inside A Heart 1

A World Of Unloved Men 2

Dog On A Beach 9

Solitary Tulip 10

Oh! The Other Nine 12

What Price Must A Lonely Heart Pay 20

Mentally Castrate 21

Life Is A F---Up...28

Rustling Autumn Leaves..31

The Time Has Come...32

Oh Please Don't Ask Me 36

My Dreams Remembers You...37

Life Is But A Passing Flame 38

My Life Is In Your Hands 39

What's Life?..40

One Lifetime I've Sworn..41

A Whisper of Warm Winds...42

Good Morning Sun..43

I Travel On..44

Your Deep Down Secrets 45

The Borning Of The Day...46

The Setting Sun..47

Crimson Grey And Royal Blue.................................48

You've Found Yourself An Old Love...................49

On A Ship I Sailed One Evening 52

Tho I Made You Cry..53

The Night Was Dark And Dreary.....................54

Heart Of Mine..55

Sorry -- So Sorry So Very Sorry.....................56

To Dream In Life 58

You Never Know 60

Ode To Two Lovely Lips 61

The Lowly Grass...64

No Poppies This Year 65

---- Alone ---- 70

Oh Snowflake Cold 73

Shana I'd Like To Thank You 74

There Is Light For Me 76

If A Tree Falls...77

Women Are A Part Of Life 78

The Beauty Of A Rose.......................................79

Why Stand You So Lonely.................................81

Tiny Flower Of Spring......................................82

Thank You For Your Time 84

Dear Reader:

Come travel with me along one of life's most travelled roads yet one of life's most unknown, unseen but not forgotten. Take a visit "Inside a Heart" (page 1) and picture that incident in your youth. The unforgettable incident which, as it more so than anything else, shaped, governed and regulated ALL the rest of your times.

So make a backward trip into this "World of Unloved Men"(page 2). I'm sure you will remember that vagabond along the road you travelled, whose only sin was in trying to find the lost 90% of his life before his last claim to manhood is also cut off and cast away.

Take a walk along with me to watch the "Borning of a Day" (page 46). "Dream in Life" (page 58), always remembering that "There is Light for Me" (page 76), that there is light for ALL of US. As long as we keep fighting against that urge to give it ALL up and just try to live out our existence, as outlined in "---- ALONE ----" (page 70)...

Life -- it's all about what Inside a Heart...

Inside a Heart

Moments of doubt, lonely

Thoughts, empty feelings

Moments of despair as

A heart cries out

Silently --

These times "Inside A Heart"

CAPTURES AND REVEALS --

A man's love, fears and

Doubts, a man's grasp

To hold to his manhood

Inside a Man's Heart

A World of Unloved Men

Once as a child I asked a man

Who wiser seemed to me

What caused the look of such lost hope

Which his eyes in I could see

He looked at me so long and hard

But slowly smiled he did

That long and lost and hopeless look

Is loneliness he said

I just said 'Oh' went on my way

Content it to let by

But somehow I can ne'er forget

The look in that man's eye

I've often sat since then and thought

How loneliness must be

Yet never dreamed I'd one day share

The look of one lonely as he

How strange

How fast the years roll by

And now a man am I

I've lived and loved I've traveled far

'Cross waters land and sky

I've kept within my mind somewhere

That picture I had seen

Tho it now at times appears to me

As naught but just a dream

His face so vivid I recall

So worn and haggard stood

Between two shoulders stooping down

In weary livelihood

His arms so big so muscle bound

He must have once been strong

Returns the question to my mind

What was it brought him down

He sat so long and quietly

When I did to him speak

His voice was low and broken-down

Yet gentle warm and meek

He had no shirt upon his back

But 'round his neck was hung

A solitary handcarved name

Which he looked upon... So long upon

His eyes were hollow... Cold as death

Yet there a twinkle lay

And I could see the laughter which

Did from his eyes once play

His face so drawn it gave a look

Of an artistic photograph

Each line so deep like wounds now healed

Or like talon-like whipmarks

The years upon his lonely face

Had writ their every song

And one could wonder but not ask

What brought this great man wrong

What evil twist of fate was it

What wrong for which he paid

What thing or person from his past

That haunted now his days

In wonder deep again I sit

But this time I'm alone

The years have passed so rapidly

And I have so old grown

I've lived a full and active life

I've been a swinger free

I've enjoyed years of bachelorhood

Before marriage slowed down me

I've been a lover and a pet

A beach boy and a slave

I've done some right

I've done some wrong

Enjoyed life's treasures without a care

I found a woman... No... she found me

Is accurate more to say

A lady... Of mental high degree

Who sought to change me everyway

She gave me love in doses short

Herself she me but lent

Then softly, slowly waited there

'Til I was 'round her finger bent

Three children and a home I gave

And all else the world could give

My hopes... Desires... And my goal

To with her happy live

To feel to be the man I was

The one that in me lived

The one whom with had she but cared

Our lives would be fulfilled

She took my all my everything

My love my hopes my pride

Then laughed at me and turned away

She my manhood cast aside

No more a man in mental state

I saw my life fall down

First hopes and dreams, next job and home

Then pride itself... outbound

No longer prideful as a man

In low defeat I lie

My use is now but in my strength

To pay for all she'll buy

In furs and mink in fancy cars

In planes and trains each week

I see her only as we pass

She there me on the street

And yet deep down inside I know

My love for her lives on

E'en tho she cares but to ridicule

The man she has brought down

Yet tonight as I return

She'll look at me and smile

But deep I know it isn't real

Hasn't been for quite a while

What brought me to this spot today

Where I once met that man

I guess it's but an echo back

To answer as fate planned

For as I sit here in my thoughts

It seems I hear again

The question soft I asked before

Of that beaten - broken lonely man

But strange it is as I look up

It's to me the child doth speak

"Sir, what caused the look of such lost hope

Which in your face I see"

I could not help but give a smile

As quick my thoughts retraced

The years and times right back to

This solitary place

Another time... Another man...

Another life like mine

All passing in the stream of life

Caught on the comet time

"It's life I guess my son" I said

"Which soon you'll come to find

But pray you find the happy side

Mine was the lonely side

And if you have a moment spare

To sit awhile with me

I'll gladly tell you of a boy

Once happy and young like thee"

The boy he sat with eyes so wide

To hear the story told

This same old story of my past

Which you do now behold

Then as I finished and he left

I saw on his cheek a tear

He walked so lightly 'long life's way

He filled my heart with fear

For he it seemed I saw within

Again as I had been

A dreamer seeking happiness

In the lonely world of unloved men...

Dog On a Beach...

Today...

Today as I walked along

The beach serene

No thoughts to cares

Gave I

As water lapped

Along the shore

I slowly passed it by...

I placed my foot

Upon the sand

And glanced around awhile

Thought back

To a kindly man

Another scene, another time

Then slowly -- slowly

I wandered on

As on my feet

The waters fell

Music sweet

To my sharp ears

Tho a dog's tongue

Of it can ne'er tell.

Solitary Tulip

Today a solitary tulip bloomed

In a thousand square foot land

To shout the words of life's victory

And of freedom unto man

From tiny seed to closed red bulb

Six red capes so engrossed

Paid notice not to outside world

Nor to the bees that crossed

But finally as if waiting there

For its honey spot to be

Full ready for my self own sight

As if waiting there for me

It opened and its gold content

So finely intertwined

That the crimson red which bound it round

'Twas alternated line for line

Like someone who in love did knit

Or weave with thought unmoved

Each tiny thread of gold and red

Measured for each groove

Inside six tall black stalwarts stand

As knights 'round queens of old

So steadfast to protect and guard

The treasure of honey gold

In places where one cannot see

As when a woman's passed

There came to me a perfume sweet

Which the tulip had amassed

I gazed so long intent upon

The flower I failed to see

The day 'twas changing into night

As the tulip bowed to me

Unknowing and without a dream

That to a flower I would talk

I'd chatted here for hours on end

Interrupted in my walk

What joy I'd found I 'lone will know

As tonight with pen I'll rest

And paint in words of poetic thought

These moments which by I'm blest

Oh! the Other Nine...

Oh! The other nine,

Oh heart The other nine

Let not me not be troubled

As down life's path we go

We have but just one life to live

One set of seeds to sow

Condemn not me if I should find

That my time demands of me

To seek out strangers in the night

On life's tempestuous sea

Do not take me to task I say

If you don't understand

My needs so different are from yours

My needs just as a man

I cannot see wherein you doth grieve

If my all I give to you

If I can offer so much more

Than is wanted e'er by you

What then should I in deep solitude

For hours for days for weeks

Do with this flame that's burning bright

Which of, you shame to speak

And what should I as a man do

Pray tell me 'er time is past

I can only for a time from my desires fast

If I give all that you desire

And have excess full score

What wrongs there be if then I feel

To give out even more

You like a vessel overflow until you beg no more

Your needs to mine are ten to one

Mine ten I need much more

Thus heart I find you satisfy

To use but one of mine

While I must sit in solitude

And lay waste the other nine

Such waste I fail to comprehend

When there is so much want

By others willing yet to take

Waste... You look upon with scorn

You take your one then sit you by

And gloat it does appear

With knowing smirk and hurtful mirth

As I must my nine cast away

So heart for years we lived

As I content you ne'er to shame

Lived in my world of wasted wants

E'er conscious of my pains

Oh heart... You I cared not to harm

Nor bring to ridicule

Not seeing that of me you thought

As nothing but a fool

You live it seems but to enjoy

Your status as you stand

To have me humbly beg to you

To keep me down as man

You knew oh heart that I was weak

And on this you did play

To dangle just 'nough wants for you

To ever let me stay

I cannot live without you heart

And this you surely know

Yet you push me to seek other ways

Or places to to go

I no more see why you should feel

If I can find out there

Cheated or left out or deprived

If I chose to give away

The excess which for you don't care

I sense you should not feel someway

That you have been deprived

If someone else accepts the nine

Which by you is now despised

So many hungry hungry souls

Live on and on each day

Contented they would be I'm sure

With what you cast away

The lone and lonely sick and weak

The old, the young, infirm

The wretched and forgotten ones

All for your excesses they do yearn

No change to me oh heart they seek

No thing from you they ask

Except your unwanted garbage waste

Oh heart do not take task

Oh heart I love you constantly

And so evermore shall do

But tell me what you want from me

What more heart can I do

I live for you my every breath

My thoughts all night and day

'Tis but to hold you ever near

And have you near me stay

And so dear heart I find that this

Is what my troubles bring

It seems I want you nine times more

Than you do me my love

My everything

So heart

Here in my solitude at work

At home at play

I find myself casting out in waste

Your excesses every day

Oh why did we so different fall

That you should find such joy

To see me need and want you heart

While you with me only toy

Oh why can't I e'en now

Stand firm

And do as I so should

And share the nine you push aside

With those waiting hungrily

Bad or good oh heart

I see no strings attached

I feel no chains that bind

Then why can't I go out and share

With the needy lives like mine

Perhaps in time you may turn about

And need the excess in me

Is this the hope I must live on with

As my desires alone I free

Or mayhap one day I will find

The courage and the nerve

To leave and live my needs that be

Return for you single serve

One out of ten yet here I lie

With you held in my arms

Full knowing well that oh too soon

You'll turn off cold your charms

Then once again in solitude

I'll sit and think of you

And slowly, softly,faithfully

Your unwanted nine outspew

Oh heart it seems like such a waste

Of body mind and life

To waste unwanted such energies

Which should fulfill a life

But then alas it seems that life

Is not on our needs just made

I live oh heart to keep you content

And pay for wrongs that others made

I know you see oh heart

Why you mistreat me e'er this way

You seek revenge for childhood wrongs

Against me as man each day

So beat on heart I understand

Or dear heart at least I'll try

But ever I will keep the hope

One day your doubts to rectify

For heart I love you and I know

You love and would be mine

If only in your doubtfilled thoughts

We could but share

The other nine

The other nine

The other nine

Which I in solitude must so oft cast aside

Will ever be there oh heart of mine

One day you to fill with pride

Then onwards thru our lives

Dear heart

We'll walk on hand in hand

You proud to beat within a breast of me

Of me as man

No longer then shall excess be

Nor waste that you cast out

No more desires wants nor needs

To each day uselessly cast out

No more the feel to look aside

For deep fulfillment true

But rather life's contented bliss

Each day and night with you

Oh heart beat on you fragile bird

Your childlike sounds produce

So soft and sweet inside of me

The promise of a truce

The hope of your constant sounds

Your unrevenge filled love

Your warmth your welcome spoken loud

To me forevermore from now...

What Price Must a Lonely Heart Pay

What price must a lonely heart pay?

And for what must it be paid?

How many tears does a broken heart hold?

'Til it weeps out everywhere?

What joys and hopes must shattered be?

Before eternal rest it knows

I knew not, Cared not, thought not

Of these not long ago

Then my life was torn asunder,

My hopes and dreams all died

My tear filled heart was overfilled,

With my sorrows multiplied

I longed for peace and comfort,

I ached for deaths relief

But each day brought new sorrow,

Each lonely night new grief

The price I pay is high friend

The stakes I hold are small

There cannot be a likeliness

Of happiness at all

I dream in my room so cell-like

Alone here in the crowd

I know not whom to turn to

As my heart cries out aloud ———

<u>Mentally Castrate...</u>

Ah! But alas my love

Thou shalt not me castrate

Thy charms

Shall not my life surround

Nor thy wishes make my bed

Thy little whims

Not serve to inflict

Wounds about my heart

Or head

I shall not let thee

Nor thy love

Ensnare my heart my pet

For too long e'er this

I've endured

With self-pride

Belief -- Respect.

I hold no malice love

For thee

No sorrow of times spent

Instead a warming memory

Is what by my thoughts

Are bent

But Ah!

Alas! a man I am

Have been my love

And straight

And so again I offer this

Thou shalt not me castrate

Thy mental ways

Unknown to thee

Are as of olden times

I've seen

Are as of women past

I've wooed upon

In other places

That I've been

No harm meant they

To cause or give

No grief, no pain, no worry

As to mentally destroy

They tried

With no thoughts

To Cupid's flurry.

Alas they tried

To conquer all

Like knights

In shining armour

To gain full right

In victory

Of nights shared

In deepest amore

To move the shield

That heavy lay

O'er the front arm

Of the knight

To slowly too remove

His coat

His horse — His sword

His spear of might

'Til they have standing

In his stead

With head bowed low

And defeated

A broken, waiting

Patient one

By whose meekness

They're elated.

So sorry ladies do I be

But this I cannot grasp

I cannot — did not

Will not bend

To the timely whims

Of any lass

And so I like the wind

Or seas

Shall roar loud in joy

In love or hate

And walk alone

'Til one I find

Who will not me

Mentally castrate

I hold no regrets

From you oh love

Instead 'tis but

A loving feeling

Which with I write

This fond adieu

As from thy life

I'm leaving

Perhaps in time again

We two

Shall pass or meet

And ponder

But what you had a chance

To keep

In life's ocean

You've pushed under

Three times I called

Into your life

And three times

To your hearts door

A-seeking but to enter in

But now I'll call

No nevermore

For time love's

But a moving thing

In past we've seen it fly

Too late we grasp

For moments gone

So uselessly we try.

My thoughts go back

To fonder times

To laughter

Gay and jolly

When time in life

You found to spend

In sharing bits of life

So fully

Then deep your thoughts

It seems alas

Have gone to seek

Their fate

To bargain

With all you did give

Whilst mentally

Me, you do castrate

I said before

I shall not be

E'er but the man I am

So take me — leave me —

Love or hate me

But still

What I am I am.

So love in closing

You may see

Why to your wishes

I can't bend

I'll be your man

Or lover full

Not content with

Now and then

I cannot — will not

Cast myself

To moments of life

You'll give

I have too much

To do in life

To await those moments

You would live

My heart it hurts

My dreams have dimmed

But I leave you

Even as I came

With pride — respect

With hopes intact

Tho I've lost

One of life's games

My lost however

But mental was

As once again my mind

Thinks straight

'Tis better to have

A hoped love lost

Than win as

As a mentally Castrate.

Life Is a F---up...

So often I will think of you

Of you

Of things past

And times gone

I see you in every face

Tho I know quite well

You're gone

No one can reason

Why I smile

As I gaze out into space

It's only 'cause

Even out there

Stands a picture

Of your face

Your form — your figure

And your way

Of tossing light your hair

The ringlike curls

Which fluttered down

Like feathers thru the air

Your little warm

And cheerfilled laugh

Your everything I guess

Brings joy to me

Tho in memory

Alone know I this happiness

As they say

We all twins have

And yours I guess

I've found

But each time

That she is near

It feels like you're around

And tho she never love

Will know

Why her presence

Makes me smile

It's nice again

You to see near

Even for just a little while

For truly

As they've often said

Love leaves 'fore its found

So I know love

But much too late

I miss your not being 'round

So as I sit and gaze

I think

As she slowly walks me by

But for the smiles

You gave to me

Well Sweetheart I'd sit

Alone and cry

For surely as you remarked

The day my heart fell

From love's cup

As you lay that last time

In my arms

'Yes life' "Life is a f---up".

Rustling Autumn Leaves

Rustling Autumn leaves on yonder mountain

Children swinging Indian Summer away

Last grass cutting of the season blowing

O'er ground still wet from rain of yesterday

Shadows now long at three is falling

From trees and people as they lazily move

Watching without anticipation the evening

So early now following the afternoon

Lines across the river try for finals

As Winter's chill soon back will push the fish

While shag coats on the dogs are growing

As they sniff the trees and the picnic dish

Shouts and screams and loud dronings

Break the silence in full constant streams

As life invades a parklike Autumn's setting

Shattering anew the chilly Autumn's breeze

Hours on end seems now so shortened

As sunup to sunset seems all but naught

We too like rustling Autumn leaves

On yonder mountain falling

Within the changes all of life are caught

The Time Has Come

The time has come

The time has come

The time, for freedom, has come

The time we waited on

The time we dreamed upon

The time of restitution for things gone

The time has come

The time -- the time -- the long awaited time

The years of suffering and woe

The years of pain, grief, sorrow

The years of bullshit slavery

Yea Bullshit slavery we took from you

Those years are gone

Those years are gone are gone and in their place

There reigns, there reigns

There reigns eternal peace

There reigns eternal freedom

There reigns eternal hope, for us

We're gonna get our due, our due

We're gonna get our rights

We're gonna walk tall, tall as black men

Equal -- equal -- equal in all ways

The time has come

The time has come

The time, for freedom, has come

The time we waited on

The time we dreamed upon

The time of restitution for things gone

The time has come

The time -- the time -- the long awaited time

The years of suffering and woe

The years of pain, grief, sorrow

The years of bullshit slavery

Yea Bullshit slavery we took from you

Those years are gone

Those years are gone are gone and in their place

There reigns, there reigns

There reigns eternal peace

There reigns eternal freedom

There reigns eternal hope, for us

We're gonna get our due, our due

We're gonna get our rights

We're gonna walk tall, tall as black men

Equal -- equal -- equal in all ways

But one

Equal in thoughts, in work, in plays

Equal in dreams, in schemes, in travel ways

Equal in all that's ours by right

Equal in all you stole away

Equal, but not like you a racist white

Equal as men should be who's right

Equal and free and forgiving -- for the time as come

The time has come

The time has come, The time has come

No more in slavery will we remain

No more exploited by you again

No more bending our heads in shame

For the time has come

The time has come

The time has come

And we are free -- are free, we are free

Our days of brainwashing at an end

Our days of looking down on our friend

Our days of messing up a brother

Our days of all the things we lacked

Our days of being 'shamed for being black

Those days are gone, are gone

The time has come

The time has come

And if you can see it

The time has come and you realize it

You know, you feel, you see,

You understand at last its come

You don't want to accept it's here

But you bigoted racist fiend

The time has come -- The time has come

The time has come

The time has come

When all my fathers days in chains

When all my mothers cries of pain

When all my childrens hurts again

You will hear -- You will hear

But now, now you'll understand

You'll understand their patient years

You'll understand their tears -- and me

Yes you'll understand even me

We must be free

'Cause we know, we now know

The time has come

Oh Please Don't Ask Me

Oh please don't ask me where I go
When I am not with you
It would break my heart to tell you
And you'd know that I'm untrue
I cannot help my feelings dear
I cannot change my ways
I only hope you'll understand
And forgive me some sweet day

For my itching feet are itchy
My roving eyes still rove
My aching arms seek strange new love
Love I've never had before
My cursed life's a ruin
But I must travel on
Forgive me please my Darling
But my will is not my own

I made to you a promise love
To always remain true
To never ever put you down
To always stand by you
I've tried my best my Darling
But you were never really mine
So I seek my own fulfillment
With each strange love I find

One day perhaps you'll wander
Upon paths that I now tread
And then perhaps you'll understand
The life that I have led
You'll realize the broken heart
And sorrow that I know
But I pray like me you won't start
Down this lonely road to go

My Dreams Remembers You

My dreams remembers you
Just like they really should
My heart calls for love you wouldn't give
You had a chance to be my love
But you were born to be Untrue
My best friend had a heart of gold
Until he found it had all been sold
I longed for you to come again
Until my heart was blue
But now my friend and I both know
You're gone and we're glad to see you go
Cause you were born to be Untrue

Life Is But a Passing Flame

Life is but a passing flame
Which we are caught upon
To live awhile —— smile awhile
Then slowly move along
It sometimes opens forth a rose
To fill our darker days
To take away the weary toil
In sweet and gentle ways
At other times it sends a smile
Or the touch of someone's hand
To lift the lonely spirit up
In a far or distant land
Yet then again at times I've seen
The best of dreams come true
Tho only for a little while
It's heavenly what they do
And so friend dear in passing by
May these few lines of mine
Say thank you for a day recalled
From these memories of mine
And tho we may never meet again
Through life you can be sure
A friend is here if e'er you need
One to stand steadfast by you

My Life Is in Your Hands

My life is in your hands

My love is in your care

My dreams know no other bands

My mind has thoughts no other can bear

'Cause no one loves you like I do

You pilot my ship 'cross the waters

You give me the strength to go on

You save my heart from needless slaughter

You're the memory of my dream every morn

Still no one loves you like I do

We are happy young and carefree

We are joyous all year round

We hold each other's love reverently

We speak not of another or go along

Yet no one loves you like I do

Because I found you in my dreams

And I hold you in my mind

And I place you in my every scheme

You are just a vision no one can ever find

That's why no one loves you like I do

What's Life?

What's life?

Have you ever stopped and wondered

Has your empty heart ever pondered

Are there deep memories you remember

That's Life………

What's Love?

Didn't you ever stop and ask out

What your loneliness is all about

What makes you feel to cry or shout

That's Love………

What's Hope?

Has your heart ever felt anxious

Have you waited for someone precious

Have you dreams you would keep from us

That's Hope………

What's Hurt?

Have you heard a poor heart breaking

Or an orphan for its mother crying

Or of Christ on Calvary's cross dying

That's Hurt………

What's Forgiveness?

Have you been reconciled to a lost friend

Do you believe in a world without end

Do you feel God would take you back again

That's Forgiveness………

What's Life?

Its love its hope its hurt too

Its forgiveness to give or receive anew

Or to let us pass so deadly through

That's Life.........

One Lifetime I've Sworn

One lifetime I've sworn to serve you

One chance to be so free

One time to seek and find you

One who could stand by me

One idea of life's journey

One which we all must make

One road to joy or loneliness

One time alone to take

One love to be eternal

One girl to be your own

One chance to find true happiness

One chance to turn it down

Oh fool oh fool please listen now

Before it is too late

One day I'll beat no longer

One day you'll see me break

A Whisper of Warm Winds

A whisper of warm winds

A glimmer of light

Smiles on bright faces morning to night

A chill on the night wind

Tho a clear full moon glows

O'er green grassy fields now

Where fresh flowers grows

A tingle of raindrops

With no mixture of ice

No frost on our windows

Makes this place so nice

Birds singing sweetly

In the full treetops above

Assures us of Springtime

Fills our lives with new love

People are smiling

Umbrellas are few

Boats and convertibles

Now sparkle anew

'Tis funny that weather

Makes of life such a change

Yet people ignore it

My aren't people strange?

Good Morning Sun

Good morning Sun of Sunday morn

Your face 'tis good to see

Your reddish Golden hue is borne

O'er e'en this foggy sea

You glimmer brightly tho so far

Your warmth still tries to fill

Each empty hollow nook and lair

Removing nights cold chill

The foggy dawn doth pass on by

As birds cross thru the grey

So softly they do onwards fly

To greet you Sun today

So may our lives in love go on

Thru bright or foggy day

And help us as our lives are cast

Whilst on these tides we be

To look e'er for your Golden hue

O'er hill and foggy sea

And so dear Sun on Sunday morn

We will in wonder gaze

At beauty pure as day moves on

And you clear this foggy haze

I Travel On

As the morning breaks in gold upon the seashore

Sending glimmering streaks across the silent waves

As the hills and trees reflect upon the new day

Tranquility and peace seems to be near

See the clouds go scurrying 'cross the blue sky

See the Autumn's gold on the Summer's green

See the flocks of birds high in South flight

See the beauty everywhere plain to be seen

Feel the touch of Winter's cold breath blowing

Watch the ships sail softly o'er endless seas,

Touch the warm warm hand of your loved one

Come along enjoy this whole world with me

I may only travel here a short while

Then back again another way I'll go

Tho my heart it may long to see you

To travel on is the only truth I know

I travel on I travel on travel ever on and on

I travel on I travel on travel ever ever on and on

To distant shores where the warm sun stayeth

To foreign lands where Winter's all they know

To lands removed from sea and salty breezes

To desert lands or wartorn lands I go

To islands small and to islands lovely

To flats or hills or to the mountains tall

To countries lands and to vast continents

Ever on I travel in answer to life's call

I travel on travel on travel ever on and on

I travel on I travel on travel ever ever on and on

Your Deep Down Secrets

In all the time I've sailed upon

The seas of turquoise clear

I doubt that I did ever try

To understand deep down there

What lurks deep pray in you yonder

Where light ne'er enters dark

'Tis funny now that I wonder

'Bout this least of all my larks

But somehow lately it became

To me a burning thing

To find your deep down secrets

To know of you everything

So please release to me awhile

Those secrets you keep lock

Then my mind will understand you too

From wavelet to deepest rock

The Borning of the Day

The borning of the day is gone

As you we gaze upon

We wait once more for your return

When us you awake at dawn

You show the splendour of the seas

The hills and the mountainsides

You paint the clouds or so it seems

As you plate with gold the tides

Each dark cloud now a lining has

Of red, silver, or gold

And the wavelets they all sparkle bright

As your splendour they behold

And far away in another land

You brighten once again

The many hearts all waiting there

For you the friend of men

Then tho far on the other side

The night begins to fall

I cannot will not let it bring

My spirits down at all

But rather in my vision clear

I'll recall and there behold

The splendour of you Setting Sun

Which paints the eve with gold

The Setting Sun

The Setting Sun

Brings back fond Memories

Of days gone by

Of things that used to be

The Setting Sun brings back fond memories

But this I know

Of this I'm sure

The Setting Sun

That old Setting Sun

Won't bring those good days

Back to me

Here on the sea

Its evening time again

My thoughts they go

A-drifting home again

The Setting Sun

It's saying goodnight you see

But this I know

Of this I'm sure

That Setting Sun

That old and aged setting Sun

That Setting Sun

Won't bring those good days back to me

Crimson Grey and Royal Blue

Crimson grey and royal blue

You paint the world around

In soft and clear and lasting hue

When Sun you doth go down

You ring the mountains all around

With beauty pure to see

You silver line each cloud that bounds

'Bove the still and silent sea

The wavelets seem to stay awhile

To render you respect

As your magical colours fall

Their dark spots to correct

You give again to man each time

Something for which to live

In hopeful faithful waiting

'Til a new day you do give

Each heart reckons at each day

That starts anew with you

That long as they can see your face

They'll live the whole day through

And when you to your slumber goes

Recalling your picturesque scene

You leave the night for deeper thought

Of things deep and serene
Lastly to the lonely heart
You bring a beauty's love
You show there's beauty on this earth
As you spread it from above
Crimson, grey and royal blue
You paint the world around
In soft and clear and lasting hue
Each day Sun as you go down

You've Found Yourself an Old Love

Herein I'll always remember you in song
You've found yourself an old love dear
That's free and warm and true
A time of joy while he holds you near
And I'm so glad for you
You never should have let me love
The way I loved you dear
And you never would have had like now
To try to hide your inner fear
Tho I love you and I always will
There's something you should know
I'll live quite at peace contentedly
Even tho I'll miss you so

For you've given me my Darling
Reasons to live that make life real
So don't feel bad within yourself
For the way that I now feel
You gave me a smile so tender
That day when first we met
And friendship warm and needed
So how can I regret
It blossomed into something
We both know can't go on
And I'm sorry if I've hurt you
But our love it wasn't wrong
You've given me renewed hope love
To seek my saviour's face
I hide my face no longer now
In shame and in disgrace
So I hope your love will linger
For me deep in your heart
For tho you're gone away from me
I'll remember you in song
Somewhere beyond the blue,
I'll find a mansion in the sky
For the good times we have known
I can't bring myself to say goodbye

Tho you don't want me now

In my heart you'll always be

For I can't stop loving you

You mean all the world to me

Forgive me forgive me

Less I pass not here again

To have known you and to have loved you

I'm a happy happy man

And as you tread on life's pathway

May the Good Lord bless and keep you

Safe in the arms of Jesus

Its a sin How I love you

So lets say goodbye like we said hello

If that's all that's left of love

What a friend we have in Jesus

He, touched my heart with your love

Here in the Blue Canadian Rockies

We shall sing a sad refrain

Somewhere my love, I'll wait for you

'Til we meet again, anytime

I may never get to heaven

This is my life, I realize

So I'll travel on, until, the end,

With memories, forever, Pretty Blue Eyes

On a Ship I Sailed One Evening

On a ship I sailed one evening

For the pleasure of the day

Enjoying all the peoples passing by

Then there came a face that I knew

Would be by my side someday

If I didn't let my chance now go by

So as she sat there all alone

With a cup pressed in her hands

I walked up and introduced myself

Wondering what would happen now

If on my lonely ways I'd gone

Not knowing more about her everyday

But -- I look back contentedly

Even tho the times have passed

And the warm glow now she tries to hide

For I know we both knew happiness

When she was standing by my side

But from me now I know she'll go

As in a world alone she cares to stray

Tho life'll be miserable now she's gone

A sorrow I'd hoped to never know

Yet one day 'til be — 'cause that's life

To live to like to love for just a while

One day mayhap she'll come share my life

And happy days will be mine again

So 'til that day draws nigh to me

In my heart she'll always be

A memory of a precious love I knew

Tho she's gone away, her warmth remains

To warm my heart, my soul my memories

Tho I Made You Cry

Tho I made you cry tho I broke your heart

Please don't leave me here all alone

You can see I love you lets make another start

Won't you say that you'll be mine my own

I'm regretting — regretting — regretting

I know that I'm sorry for the things that I said

Wont you give your love to me forever

If you leave me now I'd take my life instead

Than to try to live without you any longer

While I'm regretting — regretting — regretting

So Darling Darl ng say that you'll be mine

Tell me that you love me and no other

Show me you are mine

You know that I am thine

Let our love go on and on forever

The Night Was Dark and Dreary

The night was dark and dreary

As on the ship I sailed

Going back through my memories

To days afore this letter you mailed

To days and nights we wandered

Along the sea washed sands

To times we sat and pondered

In a far better distant land

Then you used to be my darling

And made my life of warm charms

At each days start and ending

You were here in my arms

But alas the years have gone on

Your love now has all run out

As I sit reading your last letter

As those old times I think about

You say sweetheart that it's best

For us no longer to go on

You say you're sorry but our test

Is but another we've failed upon

You're asking for your freedom

To live and love anew

You're asking me to forgive

And to forget my love for you

So I will sail forever onwards

Wherever the tide doth flow

Hoping one day it'll take me homeward

Where our love did one time grow

I'll love you Darling always

That's why I now set you free

And tho you're gone upon your ways

You'll remain here in my memories

Heart of Mine

Heart of mine

O'erwroth you be

Let silence end

Loves games suspend

Your touch

But once to feel

If you can but a message see

Long flowing on the wind

On mountains high or lowly limb

Via every breeze that's blowing

Entering every hidden nook

Yet for rest never staying

Onwards to its destiny

Utopia

Never knowing

Sorry -- So Sorry So Very Sorry

Sorry — so sorry so very sorry

Your cold cold heart can't see

Regretful and lonely and so sorry

You don't share true love for me

You've never ever ever been alone

You always want just a way your own

You will not give of yourself alone

I'm sorry that you I couldn't own

I love you but you are mad

I want you but you're so sad

I hope one day your heart will find

You love someone like this love of mine

You tore me apart from friend and family

I gave up all to try to make life happy

You gave me shame and heartaches great

And tho you blame me dear I'll wait

'Cause you still mean life to me

"You can't set me free"

Whatever I do I'll always love you

So I've tried and I'll try to convince you

No one can judge whats right or wrong

No one can call back love that's gone

But true love never seeks to flee

And true love you never had for me

You wanted you a security seal

You didn't want a love that's real

You needed a man to prove you alive

But you died inside when you bore the child

You feel now you've got it made

If you were woman at all you'd be ashamed

But what you're born you'll live and die

And the streets are calling you 'tis no lie

So you go on I'll wait for you

'Cause my love for you at least is true

To Dream in Life

To dream is to hold to life
To live is to have held a dream
To die is to lose it all
Or so at least to me it seems
Life you never ever end
As long as a dream I hold
Leaving youth no nearer eternity
I travel ever seeking your goal
Why can time pass us by
With no ode to sing but blues
E'en our dreams so quickly fly
Chasing after lost loves untrue
Onwards do I chase in wonder
Every hope that comes anew
Every dream that drives me yonder
To my end my goal my you
I have tried to find a reason
For the paths which I have crossed
Each new dream a new lost person
Yet ne'er replacing one's that's lost
Oh life you'll ne'er ne'er end
Yet you hold me as your own
Telling me you are a friend
One whom with I must go on

Lastly you need now eternal

What I have to help you on

Tho you chase my dream forever

You without me can't go on

Thus I live and dream and love

You oh life tho cruel you be

Seeking e'er to hold me empty

Never 'ever to set me free

Now alas a dream appears here

Where no dream appeared before

One more chance maybe to free be

If your hand I can but hold

You like a dream so far away

Fills my heart my soul and mind

Wondering if perchance someday

You could be a dream of mine

Life tho you never 'ever end

But this time hold back your sting

Let come true this dream for me life

Then for you I'll do anything

Like a youth now new enduring

Like the kiss of Summer's breeze

Love yet new yet never ending

Flowing warm like Summer Seas

You Never Know

When morning breaks with rosy light
And the cold of night is gone
Do you wonder at the new days beauty
Or is it a scene in passing time
What are the thoughts that binds your eyes
In such a steadfast gaze at life
That makes your being e'er respond
To word or pain or touch
You know not
Is life not then but a passing day
Whereon we all are caught fast
Reliving each experience past
Regretting each memory gone on
And yet Yes friend you and I
It seems we still travel on
Content our full day to live out
Intent it'll be all our own
Oh selfish, foolish egotistical self
What are we to become
We who cannot e'en explain ourselves
Doth try to, to the others turn
With words of wisdom

Fear or threat

With deep depressing qualms

We move from morning into night

From life into deaths arms

Alas 'tis then we find if ever

That our days end is nigh

We've lived it yes

But as fate would

Not changed by you nor I

Ode to Two Lovely Lips

If I lean against a bough of oak

And so softly speak your name

Would you look on me as passive man

Would you look on me in shame

If I climb the highest hilltop

And I lean over valleys ground

To shout your name in hill and dale

Would you think to put me down

If I caught the passing sparrow

Gave it soft voice of the dove

Would you let it speak once for me

Like a whisper from above

If I lean to touch the lily

As by babbling brook it grew

And passed your name upon it

Would it e'er be heard by you

If I wrote a thousand verses

As I lean by yonder wall

In each one your name embracing

Would you still reject them all

Just a name so small but given

Each of us to make unique

A media which once but spoken

Brings message from one who speaks

To differentiate from the others

What one to us would say

In a complimentary gesture

Tho but passing life's highway

So to your form I gaze at splendour

From your soft hair to your feet

From the tips of soft warm fingers

To your pearl-like cultured teeth

In your eyes glow brightly shining

O'er a nose perfection of

To a mouth which without speaking

Tells of hidden sensuous love

Yet thru a l the most outstanding

As but once me by you slip

I gaze in wonder long upon

Your most perfect rosy lips

Lips which so like a rosebud

Can from tight close to open be

From locked honey-holding vessel

To warm words, laughter carefree

From seeming pout to whisper

Or from shout to silent smile

From slightly ope' tantalizing

To tongue touched so light awhile

In shape and fullness given

As complete a pair as seen

On any painted portrait

Or on any movie screen

That's why I gaze in splendour

As I lean and at you look

With whatever is near supporting

Oak -- hill -- dove -- wall or brook

So if I lean against a bough of oak

And so softly speak your name

It's a tribute to your beauty fair

Lovely lips full wild untame

The Lowly Grass

Just a few blades of grass that's all

And yet to me they're companions too

They seem to be so friendly and warm

And stick so close in all they do

Each blade is different in some way

Yet each entwines in warm brotherhood

Bending with the wind now everyway

Together strengthening the baseroots good

While walking over them one can almost see

Their unity in springing upright back

Their uniformity is a thing to me

Which as yet we all do grossly lack

Ah yes — even the lowly grass

Can seem to teach us how to get along

But alas we let their advice pass

As our egotistic ways we go on

But the grass it welcomes all the rain

The Summer sun and winds that blow

Taking each season as it comes again

Assured by some power we do not know

We work and plan and strive and try

To get ahead of our fellowman

To find only that life has passed by

Throwing age into our best laid plan

Oh why cant we to nature return

From the lowly grass a lesson get

Open up our lost minds and learn

Before we perish here in our deep regret

No Poppies This Year

I'll buy no poppies this poppy day

Haven't bought them for many a year

I'll buy no poppies this poppy day

And my reason is simply "I care"

I care for a man who once went to war

Watched as friends suffered and died

I care for a man who for years endured

While dying in anguish inside

I care for a veteran who is long forgot

A war casualty like all the rest

I care for a spirit broken and beat

Which walked tall with all of the best

I care for a heart that once did believe

In the right for which he once fought

I care for a heart now broken in grief

Seeing the fight really was all for naught

No I'll buy no poppies this poppy day

Haven't bought them for many a year

I'll buy no poppies this poppy day

And my reason is simply "I care"

———————

I'll wear no poppies this poppy day

You may call me whatever you will

I'll wear no poppies this poppy day

In respect for one suffering still

In respect and remembrance of a tall man

Who for his country did offer his all

Not knowing or seeing as he forward went

The realities behind the war call

In respect for a man without a name

Not a number or mark did they keep

Just a finger to place on a trigger to pull

To insure their full freedom they'd keep

In respect to a man like others he knew

Who lived under the colonial's heel

Men who died unknown, unremembered, unmarked

For less than human so long was their deal

I'll wear no poppies this poppy day

You may call me whatever you will

I'll wear no poppies this poppy day

In respect for one suffering still

———————

I'll salute no flagstaff this poppy day

No time I of silence shall keep

For four hundred years of Silence I've known

Now no more silent will I let you sleep

Awake you who mourn for the wounded and dead

Those you in the last wars did lose

Pause awhile in your sorrow and think instead

Of those you've ruined with dope and with booze

Think of those who died in the trenches cold

Those who often spearheaded the attack

Those your Governments failed to in register hold

Because unlike you their skins were all black

Think of the reasons the enemy you fought

That a nations Sovereignty be not usurped

Then think of the nations under colonials rule

Of its peoples anguish, pains and its hurts

I'll salute no flagstaff this poppy day

No time I of silence shall keep

For four hundred years of Silence I've known

Now no more silent will I let you sleep

———

I'll offer no prayers on this poppy day

Save one that your throne shall downfall

I'll offer no prayers on this poppy day

Nor again 'til my peoples freed all

No prayers from this section will come

No feelings of sorrow, pain or regrets

No bugle, no trumpet, no taps no drum

No recognition from me will you get

For living and breathing there is a man

Who survived where others had died

Who believed "Nothing would be too good"

after the war

Lived six years believing your lies

A tall man who thought when the war was thru

And your freedom again secure lay

Then you by your promise would free him too

Yet still under your yoke does he stay

So I'll buy no poppies this poppy day

Haven't bought them for many a year

I'll buy no poppies this poppy day

In respect for my father so dear

———

No poppies for me no flag to salute

No prayers and no silence to share

No grief for your dead and wounded have I

For no recognition to my peoples you gave

So look me upon with deep scornful eye

When Remembrance Day it draws nigh

I too am remembering someone I knew

Whom you've broken and often let cry

I too shall remember the years he did give

Thou you failed e'en to mark down his name

Like so many others of his race and kin

You for his skins shade made him ashamed

You promised in lies like you've always dealth

His freedom for self and for land

But once you your freedom saw resecured

He again became just a Black man

So sell me no poppies this poppy day

Ask me not in your prayers to bend head

For no tribute I owe to your wounded or lost

When I think of my unlisted dead

Nay no tribute I owe to your wounded or lost

When I think of my father your living dead

... Al my living dead

---- **Alone** ----

The easiest decision we can ever make in life is to be
ALONE

ALONE we have no one to depend on us,

no one to worry about us, no one to care for us,

no one to wait on or to need us.

ALONE we can justify being lazy, smart, right, wrong,

good, bad, crazy, sane, clean, dirty, happy, sad,

loved, lonely, joyfilled or miserable.

ALONE we can tell ourselves all that we would have liked

was beyond our reach and our abilities to ever hope to

obtain though we never tried nor took a chance at it.

ALONE we can convince ourselves of all the end results

of each and every beautiful experience

and opportunity offered us which we rejected.

ALONE we can conclude every relationship in finality

of uselessness before it has begun

for we will never give it ground in which to grow.

ALONE we can wrap ourselves in a blanket of ice made out

of past failures, mistakes and regrets and tell ourselves

this justifies our so cold state of ALONENESS.

ALONE we need never get hurt, be in love, feel cared for,
share experiences, create memories, cry, laugh, act silly,
act intelligent or just act... human, for we are ALONE.

ALONE we come and go as we please, where we please,
do as we please, with whomsoever we please knowing
we will never be tied to conventions, rules nor commitments
because we are ALONE.

ALONE we sit and watch the funny comedies of life
but need not laugh as there is no one there to share the
laughter with and as such it has only an empty hollow ring.

ALONE we set a delectable table but have no appetite save
for meager sustenance as food, though beautiful,
is so tasteless when partaken ALONE.

ALONE we open a bottle of spirits for that little single
drink but soon find we consume all its contents
trying to find a shield which we can escape behind
and so not see ourselves ALONE.

ALONE we listen to music and recall the beauty of it
but cut it short as we realize that it brings back memories
of when we were not ALONE.

ALONE we finally turn off the day though it be young
even as we did so many days before and crawl into
the safe confines of a large bed ALONE, and
toss and turn from side to side
marveling at all the empty unused space
we can now enjoy ALONE,
then we curl ourselves into a small ball
into some tiny corner of that space and
cry ourselves to sleep knowing no one will ever hear us
nor see the tears we shed as we are ALONE.

Finally sleep envelopes us giving us the truest escape
from ourselves and our lonely world by taking us
into the only realm wherefrom we can be truly ...
---- ALONE ----

ALONE... yet feel the joy, the pleasure,
the companionship of truly being... ALONE

---- **ALONE** ----
YES...

The easiest decision we can ever make in life is to be
---- ALONE ----

Oh Snowflake Cold

The cold and icy snowflakes fall

Upon the frozen ground

They flutter in their unrushed ways

'Till they blanket out the ground

The tiny grass lies waiting cold

For spring to bring it warmth

The songbird doth its chorus hold

'Till there's something to be warmed

The trees so tall all shake their heads

In awe or inspiration

As they too accept the snowflakes fall

In dread or anticipation

Yet as against the window pane

I see a child's nose pressed

I can't but help a laugh I feel

At the child's face so impressed

For though tiny and so flake soft

The snowflake tumbles down

Tho cold it warms the sad child's heart

And with a smile removes the frown

Oh snowflake cold and tiny fall

But to each of us you seem

A different vision tho big or small

Yet still you are a pleasant dream

Shana I'd Like to Thank You

Shana I'd like to thank you

For the time short we have known

For the feelings of a realness

I'd forgot that life could hold

For a full content completeness

In my heart body mind and soul

For once in my doubt filled memory

One which was my love my own

I have had and been with many

Of life's women in my time

And tho they paid lip service

Ulterior motives held their minds

In search they of name and marriage

In search they of kids and home

Fell in love 'cause I was handy

Saw me as a thing to own

Filled my time with words and actions

Hollow cold without a feel

But for once I felt just wanted

Just for once I felt love real

Shana I'd like to thank you

Tho you've gone your memory stays

Warm tender my heart in forever

Though we traverse our separate ways

For one time I saw love living

Saw it in eyes sparkle and shine

Saw it in your free abandon

While you lay gentle on my mind

Felt love as you lay beside me

Unashamed the world to show

Heard it as your friends were talking

Of the beauty of your glow

But to pay my dues it came time

Your love to bind or to set free

And I heard the fiddler playing

Born to lose it just can't be

Yet my dreams will live forever

Of the rendezvous short we shared

For my one time when with assurance

I knew someone who really cared

So Shana I'd like to thank you

And hope someday we'll meet again

If we do tho no more as lovers

Gaze your eyes on me as friend

There Is Light for Me

I've been to sleep and awakened

I tried but could not see

Then reaching for tiny switches

Thank you, there is light for me

I looked into the pitch black night

I grew afraid it seemed

Then the wind blew the clouds around

Thank you

Stars of which I'd dreamed

Thank you Sun and Moon and Stars

Thank you

Bulbs and tubes and fires

Thank you

Little fireflies that shine

Thank you, light of my desire

I've grown to really love the light

And the beauty it doth show

But there are three lights above all

That holds the brightest glow

The first is sight

God's light to us

To view creations grand

The second is the light to see

The good in our fellowman

And lastly there yet remains
A light that's bright tho small
The light of love in a friend's eyes
Must surely outshine them all

If a Tree Falls

If a tree falls in a forest with no one around,
Is there any sound?

If a heart cries ALONE for companionship in the night
How can it be heard?

If a bird had not the courage to try its wings
again and again after each fall it had taken
How would it learn to fly?

If a seed buried under the frozen ground of Winter did
not respond to the offered warmth of Springs Sun
Wherefrom would later come the Rose?

If a youthful person with all life ahead will not grasp the
hands offered to pull oneself out of the rut of selfpity, of
loneliness, of despair, of lack of self-worth,

Do not expect the offered hands to remain outstretched
forever as they too need warmth and filling
To continue their own existence...

Women Are a Part of Life

Women are a part of life
This I have come to know
But yet it seems in all life
They're but a fashion show
I've seen each kind and colour all
I've watched them tall or short
I've seen the poles and butterballs
I've seen them cry and smile and snort
I've known the brown the red the black
The white and golden-haired
I've known some that nothing lacked
And some that just didn't care
I've seen the lively sprightly ones
The quiet sad and blue types
I've seen the ones to studies gone
I've seen the gay carefree types
I've seen the soft and gentle girls
The rough and tumble tigers
I've known the poor and wayward girls
I've known the for men fighters
I've known the feminine and sweet
I've known the women libbers
I've known those that would not cheat
I've known the sly cold fibbers

So tho it seems I've known them all

At times it makes me wonder

Why each time a new one calls

Of her ways and thoughts I ponder

'Til now alas I chance to see

That their wiles are but a false show

They really are out to get me

To pick but one from their wild wild fashion show

The Beauty of a Rose

Sometimes I like to sit and gaze

At the beauty of a rose

At the way which its petals all

Seem shaped to timely fall

At the green which doth its stem embrace

As it holds up to the sky

The beauty and the fragrance of

The rose which stands for aye

Today by chance I walked along

And my eyes they happened to

Stay long upon a tulip ope'd

Such as I'd never saw

Its beauty to my mind surpassed

The beauty of the rose

As it swayed so lightly in the breeze

To send to me with ease

Its fragrance soft and beautiful

Which flowed thru all the trees

The birds sat watching in the trees

As down on the Earth I knelt

To take my time and slow caress

The tulip so softly pressed

I brought my face to inches then

Enveloped in its smell

As I became e'en more enhanced

With the tulip as I knelt

Three times I bent to pluck it off

Three times my hand withdrew

Too beautiful to cut life short

Even to share it dear with you

So here instead I've brought for you

The second choice that be

A photograph of beauty unsurpassed

Of the tulip I did see

My time my love is long your own

My life with you I'd share

So come walk awhile with me my love

That you may share this tulip rare

Why Stand You So Lonely

Why stand you so lonely
So solemn and so still
Surrounded by the little grass
Which grows on yonder hill
Why do you never tire
Of winking night and day
With you tired looking red red eyes
O'er looking many a bay
In Winter's cold in Springtime fog
Or dark dark Summer's night
In Autumn's rainy evenings too
You always watch and wait
And tho you wink your red eye
You never sleepy grow
Tell me your secret Lighthouse
It I would like to know
Are you content to guide us on
Away from harmful shores
Or show to us safe harbours
Where from the storms we go
Or is it just a lark for you
To wirk as we pass by
To show us show us your red red eye
And let our wonder spark anew

Tiny Flower of Spring

What is a tiny flower of spring

Which in beauty simple grows

Which takes the colours of nature all

And fashions therefrom its clothes

A flower which today is but a bloom

To tomorrow wither and die

One day so short to live full blown

Then leave this Earth for on high

That flower it is a message sent

To hearts and loves and men

A thought, a wish, a forgive me please

A lets try to love again

That flower is the bearer of

Our feelings deepest hid

The messenger silent competent yet

Who alone can do our bid

That flower each day is given anew

To teach to us the truth

That tho our yesterdays were sad

Today we should start anew

From garden, shop, from wayside stall

From vendor or from self

It has no meaning and its beauty's lost

If it stays alone on the shelf

To take but one or dozens bunched

Your heart will jump with joy

As you send them out to brighten up

Some lonely girl or boy

These flowers all so tiny frail

So soft and fragrance filled

Can serve to melt the hardest heart

And bring back to life love killed

Soft tiny quiet and so short

To live and share to its end

You've time yet still to use it fool

To regain your lovely friend

Or mayhap you have lost in life

One for whom you pine deep now

Send flowers to that lost loved friend

They'll tell of your lasting love

Thank You for Your Time

Thank you for your time friend

Now that you've read my lines

I feel more proud to call you friend

Since you've shared these thoughts of mine

And better yet I hope will be

The ways henceforth in which we live

As better you do comprehend

These values we try to give

My feeble ways are ancient yet

My language plain and old

Yet I hope in these Reflections

I have our story told

May somehow as you travel on

Around this changing world

You meet the incidents I've met

And love some lonely souls

May peace be yours and happiness

And lasting love yours true

And may these Reflections help

To keep that one with you

So live on friend but listen

To these last few words of mine

Now that you've read my verses

At last you see my mind

But also the mistakes I've made

Which sorrow and hurt did bring

You've seen the outcome of them now

And my ruined life of sin

So dwell on my Reflections friend

Think of me now and then

And when you feel to be a fool

STOP — Reread this book again

Thank You

Other Collections by This Author:

A Poet's Ebb And Flow

... and Touches Of Nature

In The Middle of Believe There's A Lie

Judge Me Not Without A Trial

Legends, Lives & Loves Along the Inside Passage

Love... Life's Illusive Zenith

Love's Reflections

Love's Refuge and Sonnets

Only Children Of The Universe Are We

Step Scenes Of Life

That We Too Free May Live

~ ~

For more information go to:

w w w . d n c s i t e . c a

~ ~

www.ingramcontent.com/pod-product-compliance
Lightning Source LLC
Chambersburg PA
CBHW021346090426
42742CB00008B/760